Conflict Management in the Workplace
Charles Polkey

About City & Guilds

City & Guilds is the UK's leading provider of vocational qualifications, offering over 500 awards across a wide range of industries, and progressing from entry level to the highest levels of professional achievement. With over 8500 centres in 100 countries, City & Guilds is recognised by employers worldwide for providing qualifications that offer proof of the skills they need to get the job done.

City & Guilds Group

The City & Guilds Group includes ILM (the Institute of Leadership & Management) which provides management qualifications, learning materials and membership services and NPTC (National Proficiency Tests Council) which offers land-based qualifications. City & Guilds also manages the Engineering Council Examinations on behalf of the Engineering Council.

Equal Opportunities

City & Guilds fully supports the principle of equal opportunities and we are committed to satisfying this principle in all our activities and published material. A copy of our equal opportunities policy statement 'Access to assessment' is available on our website or from the Customer Relations team.

Publications

City & Guilds publications are available from our Publications Sales department at the address below:

**City & Guilds
1 Giltspur Street
London EC1A 9DD**

www.cityandguilds.com

For general enquiries:

T +44 (0)20 7294 2468   F +44 (0)20 7294 2400

For publications enquiries:

T +44 (0)20 7294 2850   F +44 (0)20 7294 3387

First published 2005
Reprinted 2006
© 2005 The City and Guilds of London Institute
City & Guilds is a trademark of the City and Guilds of London Institute

ISBN-13: 978 0 85193 065 7
ISBN-10: 0 85193 065 4

All rights reserved. No part of this publication may be reproduced or transmitted in any form or by any means, electronic or mechanical, including photocopy, recording, or any information storage and retrieval system, without permission in writing from the publisher.

Every effort has been made to ensure that the information contained in this publication is true and correct at the time of going to press. However, City & Guilds' products and services are subject to continuous development and improvement and the right is reserved to change products and services from time to time. City & Guilds cannot accept liability for loss or damage arising from the use of information in this publication.

Cover and book design by CDT Design Ltd
Implementation by Phil Baines Studio
Illustrations by NB Illustration/Ben Hasler
Typeset in Congress Sans
Printed through Print Solutions Partnership, Wallington, Surrey

Conflict Management in the Workplace
Charles Polkey

Contents

Introduction	6

1 Assessing and reducing risk

The law relating to violence at work	9
Risk assessment Case study: The community nurse	11
Risk reduction	14
Dynamic risk assessment Case study: The suspicious person	17

2 Avoiding and defusing conflict

Responses to threat	25
Triggers and inhibitors Case study: The refused credit card	26
De-escalating responses	31
Pro-active service delivery Case study: The missed train	33
Communication – and blocks to it	42
Signalling non-aggression	49
Dealing with high-risk conflict Case study: The parking incident	52
Strategies for defusing aggressive behaviour	57
Confronting unacceptable behaviour	62
Exit strategies	64
The law relating to self-defence	65

3 Post-incident support and learning

Support for the victims Case study: The nightclub incident	69
Reporting an incident and accounting for your actions	74
Learning from what happened	76
Personal action plan	78
Helpful websites	79

Introduction

Violence and aggression within our society have steadily increased over recent years. If you are one of the many people who provide services directly to the public, you may have found yourself dealing more often with incidents involving angry and aggressive people, and you may have had to face higher levels of violence.

Training is an important element in helping staff to deal safely and effectively with clients, patients, customers and service users who may become abusive, threatening or violent. This handbook is designed to support the City & Guilds Level 2 Certificate in Conflict Management (1884), through which you will develop your understanding and skills to manage the conflict within your workplace environment.

Using this handbook
This handbook is designed to be as versatile as possible. How you use it will depend upon how your programme for the course has been designed. There are three main approaches:

1. It may be used as a pre-learning guide that you will be asked to work through before attending a classroom-based course. In this way the handbook helps you to understand the theory before practising skills and scenarios on the course itself.

2. Your tutor may decide to use it as a resource during the course – using the case studies and exercises as practical material for scenarios and group exercises during the delivery.

3. It can be used as a way of understanding the theory and revising for the exam after having attended a course for the practical elements.

It may also be used in a combination of these approaches. It contains all the information you will need to achieve the City & Guilds Certificate in Conflict Management.

Case studies
As you work through the material, your learning is supported by the use of case studies from different sectors and self-assessment exercises. The case studies are based upon real incidents that have happened to individuals working in the sector concerned. Be warned: some strong language is used, as these are real situations. Vulgar and abusive language are part of the aggressive behaviour you may meet in your workplace. The exercises are designed to help you reflect upon your learning and to put the theory into a real and practical context.

1 Assessing and reducing risk

The law relating to violence at work	9
Risk assessment **Case study: The community nurse**	11
Risk reduction	14
Dynamic risk assessment **Case study: The suspicious person**	17

Conflict Management in the Workplace

Outcome 1

Outcome 1 of the City & Guilds Level 2 Certificate in Conflict Management is set out below. It spells out what you need to do and what you need to know to successfully complete this part of the qualification.

Outcome 1
Assess and reduce the risk of violence in the work environment

What you need to do

- Assess the risks of violence that exist in the working environment
- Prepare and plan to reduce the risks of violence before undertaking a work activity involving specific risks
- Assess a situation, as it is developing, to identify risks of violence

What you need to know

- State the definition of work-related violence
- Describe the responsibilities of employers and employees outlined in the Health and Safety at Work Act 1974
- Explain the policy and guidance provided by the employer in relation to the risks of work-related violence
- Describe risk-reduction measures which eliminate or reduce risks
- Describe the process of dynamic risk assessment of the threat in a developing situation
- Recognise the importance of providing positive and proactive service to service users
- Explain the importance of responding calmly and politely to complaints of poor service and resolve issues promptly and fairly

1 Assessing and reducing risk

The law relating to violence at work

Not all of us work in the same kind of setting. Your workplace may be a shop, and you may deal mainly with customers. Or you may work in the reception area of a large hospital and interact mainly with patients and their families. If you're a parking attendant, the street is your workplace. What you learn in this book can be applied in all these settings.

The kinds of situations you face may differ from one workplace to another. But the official definition of what constitutes violence remains the same.

The Health and Safety Executive definition

The Health and Safety Executive (HSE) is responsible for the regulation of almost all the risks to health and safety arising from work activity in Britain. Workplace violence is defined by the Health and Safety Executive as:
Any incident in which a person is abused, threatened or assaulted in circumstances relating to their work.

The definition is quite wide and will include almost any form of abusive behaviour directed towards someone as a result of his or her work. For example, you refuse to serve someone alcohol in your bar. As you leave work this person challenges you in the car park, coming up to you and shouting: 'You're the bastard who wouldn't serve me!' This would fit within the definition.

The issues of workplace violence are covered under the general Health and Safety Legislation, which we look at in a moment. Most organisations will use the HSE definition as a starting point to:
– develop policy and guidance in relation to violence at work
– assess the risks faced by staff
– put in place training and other risk reduction measures that may be required
– set up appropriate reporting and recording procedures
– identify the sources of support needed in relation to violence at work.

In practice, the Health and Safety Executive recognises three forms of workplace violence:

1 Where a service user or other member of the public uses abusive language or behaviour towards you

2 Where a service user or other member of the public makes any threat towards you

3 Where a service user or other member of the public physically assaults you.

Health and safety legislation

There is no 'special' law that relates to workplace violence. The issue is dealt with in the same way as any other workplace hazard and falls under the relevant health and safety legislation. There are several especially important parts of this legislation.

The Health and Safety at Work Act 1974 – Section 2

Employers have a legal duty under this Act to ensure, so far as is reasonably practicable, the health, safety and welfare at work of their employees.

Employers have a statutory duty to do 'everything reasonable and practicable' to 'eradicate or minimise' the risk of harm from all hazards to health – including violence.

Where violent incidents are foreseeable employers have a duty to identify the nature and the extent of the risk and to devise measures which provide a safe workplace and a safe system of work.

Employers also have a Common Law 'Duty of Care' to others and are required to conduct their undertaking in such a way as to ensure, so far as reasonably practicable, the safety of other people who are not their employees, and to whom the premises have been made available.

The Health and Safety at Work Act 1974 – Section 7

The duty of care embraces employees as well as employers. Employees are required to 'take reasonable care for their own safety – and the safety of others – who may be affected by their actions or inaction'.

The duties placed on the employees do not reduce the responsibility of the employer to comply with his or her health and safety duties.

Risk assessment

Risk assessment is a well-established process for developing a safe working environment. The same processes are used to assess the likelihood of staff being subjected to workplace violence and the severity of danger they may face.

It is difficult to outline all the possible risks from workplace violence that might be faced by staff delivering a service to the public. General risk assessment is usually done in relation to the buildings and environments in which people work. For workplace violence, it is important to examine the role that the person is undertaking and the risks associated with the tasks and responsibilities when doing his or her job. There will be particular times, places, duties and tasks that will involve a greater risk of violence. For example, if someone has a responsibility to enforce compliance with rules or the law, then he or she is more likely to face workplace violence while doing so. Police officers and security staff spring to mind – but this will also apply to less obvious staff such as retail staff (who need to comply with age restrictions on alcohol, tobacco, knives and glue), ticket inspectors on trains, car-parking attendants and receptionists in Accident & Emergency who have to manage the queues waiting for treatment.

Case study: The community nurse

Rachel Adewale is a 31-year-old nurse working for a primary care trust. Her main role is caring for patients who need nursing care in their homes. Much of her work is routine care, and although many of her patients are elderly, she has a wide range of people of any age who she will look after on a short-term basis – often following discharge from hospital after surgery.

The practice covers an urban area on the outskirts of a large city. There are a couple of new housing estates, an area of old Victorian terraces, which are mainly flats and bed-sitters, and two blocks of 1960s flats. Rachel is part of a team of community nurses, which is based at the surgery. The nurses in the team are all female and range in age from 27 to 56 years of age. Weekend cover is provided from the team on a rota basis. All the nurses use their own vehicles to visit their patients at home.

Rachel Adewale checks her list of patients.

Rachel is on weekend rota. It is Saturday morning and she is about to undertake a normal round of home visits. She will be out for about three hours. She is visiting a number of patients who she has seen before, with the exception of one. From his notes, she knows that he is a male, aged 36 years, and he lives in one of the blocks of flats. He has been discharged from hospital following routine minor surgery, and she will be required to check and dress the wound.

Case study exercise: The community nurse

Look at the case study and write down all the risks of being abused, threatened or assaulted you can think of associated with the tasks and responsibilities that Rachel is expected to undertake as part of her job.

Risk reduction

Once the risk assessment for a role is carried out, it will highlight the main hazards faced by a person in that role. It is now important to establish ways in which these risks can be reduced or eliminated. Risk reduction measures fall into the three main categories described below.

Policy, procedures and guidance

The organisation must provide a clear statement about its policy in relation to workplace violence, and there should be clear procedures and guidelines about how tasks and situations should be undertaken and managed where risk of violence has been identified.

In 1986 Suzy Lamplugh, a 25-year-old estate agent, disappeared after she went to meet an unknown client. So far her body has not been found. However, she has been presumed murdered and legally declared dead. This tragic case, which led to the establishment of the Suzy Lamplugh Trust, highlighted the risks faced by people at work and drew attention to the fact that many people in similar situations were naive about the risks they faced. The establishment of a Workplace Violence Policy demonstrates the commitment of an employer to recognise and deal with the issues. This policy provides procedures and guidance to employees and establishes safe working practices designed to minimise the risks faced.

Physical measures

There is a wide range of physical measures that can be introduced to reduce risk.

Equipment can be made available, which may be as simple as a personal attack alarm or as sophisticated as a setup including surveillance equipment, cameras and specialist locks, bolts and time-locked safes. Stab-proof vests are a good example of a physical measure, but this kind of equipment almost invariably leads to a debate about its appropriateness – especially in caring organisations like hospitals and the ambulance service.

Design and layout of premises also fall within this category. For example, providing a pleasant and comfortable place for people who have to wait a long time – with refreshment facilities, reading matter and up-to-date

1 Assessing and reducing risk

information about waiting times – will help to reduce the risk of people becoming aggressive and abusive. In high-risk situations, perhaps where there is a risk of robbery or physical attack, then a place should be 'designed in' to the environment where staff can retreat safely with no possibility that the assailant can follow.

Training

Training is an important component of risk reduction and needs to be given at a level that meets the needs of the roles concerned. Everyone who faces a risk of violence should have training in recognising and reducing the risks of violence, how to respond to a situation involving conflict and how to stay safe when managing the conflict. If they are likely to face a physical assault or are expected to remove someone from the premises, then they should receive training in the physical skills to achieve such tasks effectively and safely.

Case study exercise: The community nurse

Have another look at your list of risks identified in Rachel's role. Write down the measures that could be introduced to help minimise those risks.

Dynamic risk assessment

There are many occasions when staff providing services to the public are confronted with situations which are unique and not catered for in a generic risk assessment. These are often the situations where people get hurt because they don't have a way of assessing the risks in the situation they are confronted with, and do not respond appropriately.

'Dynamic risk assessment' is a process that helps an individual to effectively assess a situation from a personal safety perspective, as it is unfolding. The person can continuously assess the circumstances and adjust his or her response to meet the risk presented moment by moment. Maybo has developed the *SAFER Approach*® to dynamic risk assessment. This continuous assessment is done in three basic stages:

1 Stepping back from the situation momentarily and making a quick assessment of the situation and the threat presented

2 Evaluating the options available to you in the light of this assessment

3 Responding by using the most appropriate option – monitoring for changes.

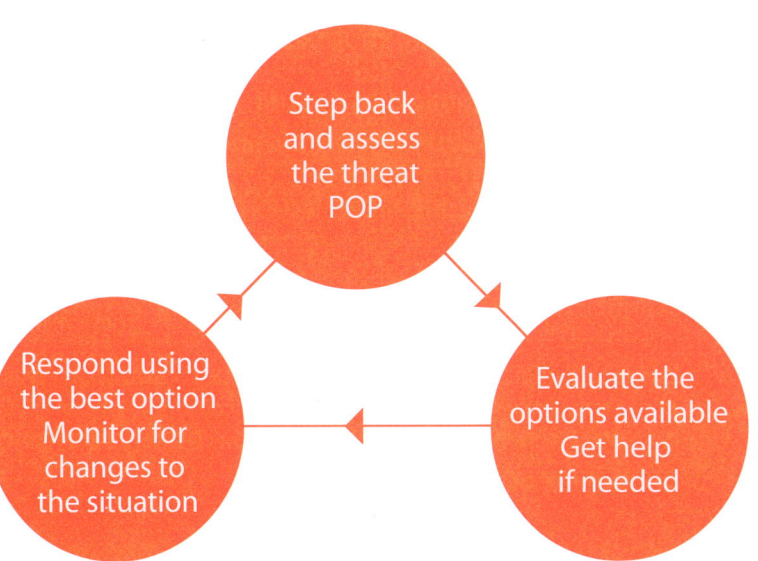

The dynamic risk assessment process.

Stepping back and assessing the threat

When making the initial assessment of the threat it is useful to use the **POP** (Person, Object, Place) method:

Person	Continually assess people to judge whether you may be at risk. If you have met the person before, what do you know about them? Do they have a history of anger or aggression? Are they a known criminal?
	If you don't know them, what can you judge from their appearance or demeanour? How do they appear? How are they dressed? Are they clean and tidy, dishevelled, dirty, unshaven? Are they suffering the effects of drink or drugs?
	Are they bigger, fitter, younger or stronger than you?
Object	Assess the situation with regard to the risk presented by any objects.
	Are there knives or other edged weapons or syringes?
	Could apparently 'innocent' articles contribute to risk – bottles or cans, glasses, ashtrays, combs, umbrellas, shopping bags, handbags, briefcases, shopping or baggage trolleys, vehicles?
Place	Assess the situation with regard to where you are – including the time of day, other people around, lighting, etc.
	Is it a noisy, hot, confined environment, a dance floor, or public area?
	Is it an isolated or poorly lit area, a staircase, or toilet?
	Is it a familiar place, such as the route to and from work?
	Is there a risk associated with certain times, such as locking or opening up premises?

1 Assessing and reducing risk

Evaluating the options available

There will be a variety of ways you could deal with the situation. An important rule is not to put yourself in a risk situation unless you have some help available or someone else knows that you are dealing with a difficult situation.

There are a variety of options available. The one you choose will depend upon the situation itself, the availability of assistance, your experience and training as to which is most appropriate:

- If you are confident that you are able to deal with the situation safely then you should do so – but continue to monitor and assess what is happening in case the situation changes.

- If you need assistance then you should not try to deal with the situation until the help arrives.

- If the situation is potentially violent and there is a risk of physical assault, then you should exit from it as soon as you can do so safely. This may not always be possible, as you have factors to consider like the safety and well being of other service users. In such cases it is important that you have been trained in calming and defusing skills and know how to prevent the situation from escalating until help arrives.

- You should only use a 'physical intervention' (holding, restraining, escorting, physical removal from premises) if you have received appropriate training in how to do it effectively, lawfully and safely.

Responding – the best option

Once you have decided upon the best way to respond, you must continue to monitor the situation and repeat the process if the situation changes.

Sally Johnson notices the man standing at the bus shelter.

Case study: The suspicious person

Sally Johnson is a shop assistant working in an off-licence store. She is 25 years old, married with two small children and she works 20 hours per week. She really enjoys the job, but she is not happy about working on her own in the store at night and her husband is very negative about her having a job – although he accepts that they need the extra money.

It's a Wednesday evening in December. During the evening, she noticed a man aged about 25 who came into the shop three times between 9.15 and 9.45 pm. On the first two occasions he stayed about five minutes looking at the wines, glancing occasionally out of the window into the street. On the last occasion he came to the counter and bought a pack of cigarettes. He was quite casually dressed, wearing a fleece, jeans and trainers, and she got the impression that he was killing time while waiting to meet someone nearby.

1 Assessing and reducing risk

It is 10.45 pm. Sally has cashed up, set the alarm and is leaving the store when she notices that the same man is standing about 50 yards down the road by a bus shelter with his hands in his fleece pockets. He glances towards Sally, staring quite intently at her, and then looks away. Her car is parked about two minutes' walk away in the opposite direction to where the man is standing. She has a mobile phone with her.

The shop is located on the High Street and there are a couple of people around, although no one is in the immediate vicinity to Sally. It is dark, drizzling with rain and the street lighting outside the shop is poor.

Case study exercise: The suspicious person

Step back and assess the threat

What are the possible situations that Sally could be facing?

Make an assessment of the threat.

Person:

Object:

Place:

Evaluate options

What are the options available to Sally?

1

2

3

4

Respond and monitor

Which response do you feel would be the most appropriate, and why?

Given your chosen response, what should Sally be monitoring to detect a change in the situation?

2 Avoiding and defusing conflict

Responses to threat	25
Triggers and inhibitors Case study: The refused credit card	26
De-escalating responses	31
Pro-active service delivery Case study: The missed train	33
Communication – and blocks to it	42
Signalling non-aggression	49
Dealing with high-risk conflict Case study: The parking incident	52
Strategies for defusing aggressive behaviour	57
Confronting unacceptable behaviour	62
Exit strategies	64
The law relating to self-defence	65

Conflict Management in the Workplace

Outcome 2

Outcome 2 of the City & Guilds Level 2 Certificate in Conflict Management is set out below. It spells out what you need to do and what you need to know to successfully complete this part of the qualification.

Outcome 2
Identify behaviour that indicates an escalation towards violence and take appropriate measures to avoid or calm and defuse the situation

What you need to do

- Use skills and behaviours which will calm and defuse the situation
- Take the appropriate action in a high-risk conflict to minimise the risk of injury to yourself and other people
- Demonstrate the skills to signal non-aggression

What you need to know

- Describe human responses to threatening situations
- Identify the most common triggers and situations where there is a risk of escalation into violence
- Choose responses which will de-escalate a potentially aggressive situation
- Describe the basic elements of communication and the blocks to communication in an aggressive or violent situation
- Describe the action to take if a situation is escalating to a high-risk conflict
- Explain how to defuse and calm a person who is behaving in an angry and aggressive way
- Choose appropriate assertive behaviour for confronting examples of unacceptable behaviour
- Describe exit strategies from potentially high-risk conflict
- Explain the law relating to self-defence

Responses to threat

Understanding and controlling our response to threat is an essential element in managing conflict. People have two mindsets or ways of dealing with a situation – the emotional (the one that feels), and the rational (the one that thinks).

These two work together, and are balanced most of the time. However, when we are particularly upset or when we feel threatened, the emotional side quickly takes over. This means that we lose much of our ability to rationalise and think clearly. When emotions surge, our balance can be tipped and the emotional mind becomes predominant. The more intense the emotion the more dominant the emotional mind becomes – and the more ineffectual the rational. In these situations we experience what has been called the 'fight or flight' response.

Fight or flight

If you are seriously threatened, your body prepares you either to stay and fight the threat or to take flight and run away from the danger. Within seconds of sensing danger, you can run faster, hit harder, see better, hear more acutely, think faster, and jump higher than you could only seconds earlier. This fight or flight response is a natural basic instinct.

We can influence whether another person decides to run away or stay and fight. We increase the chances of someone choosing to fight when we:
– invade their personal space
– continue to make them feel threatened
– block their exit path.

Triggers and inhibitors

Triggers are often small things that, when combined with other problems, spark off aggression. So if a person is already feeling frustrated by long waits, poor service, or personal circumstances, there are many triggers that will spark off a sharp reaction! You may never know what someone has been through just before their encounter with you.

Common triggers

People tend to be 'triggered' into an angry reaction if they feel:
- embarrassed
- insulted
- that they have lost face
- that people are laughing at them
- that they are not being taken seriously.

Inhibitors

You know that not everybody gets violent when they become angry. Inhibitors are things that prevent people from completely losing their temper. This is because they have inhibitions based on:
- self control (most people have a built-in control that prevents them from turning to violent behaviour)
- personal values (the way we have been brought up and the values and beliefs that we have learned may prevent us turning to violence)
- fear that the other person will fight back (most of us don't want to be hurt and realise a fight will risk this)
- social or legal consequences (these include being charged with an assault, losing one's job or licence).

2 Avoiding and defusing conflict

Case study: The refused credit card

Martin Hedges makes a call to authorise Darren Hart's credit card.

It's about 4.00 pm at the pay point in a busy electrical goods store. There is a queue of about six people and Martin Hedges, a store assistant, is operating the till. He has just had a difficult transaction which took several minutes to sort out and he realises that the next customer kept looking at his watch and sighing. Martin's view is that he can only do one thing at a time and if someone has to wait then that's life – not much he can do about it.

The next customer is Darren Hart, a white male in his early twenties. He is well built with very short hair and wearing a T-shirt and jeans. He is purchasing an MP3 player, which costs £180.

Martin apologises for the delay, but Darren merely grunts and unsmilingly offers a credit card to pay for it. Martin swipes the card and a code comes up on the till which tells him to phone the credit card company for authorisation. He says: 'I'm really sorry, but I've got to get your card authorised. It's only a quick call.' Darren is clearly unhappy about this and glares at Martin saying: 'You'd better be quick – I'm sick and tired of waiting around here. Time you got more bloody staff on when it's as busy as this.'

Martin makes the call and is told that they cannot authorise the transaction and that he must retain the card. He explains this to Darren, who begins to raise his voice saying: 'Retain it? What are you talking about? What for?'

Martin explains: 'Well, it could be for a number of reasons. It's usually because the card has been reported lost or stolen or...' Darren points his finger at Martin saying: 'Are you accusing me of being a thief? You're out of order, mate ...'

Martin quickly responds by saying: 'Not at all, sir, no. It can happen for all sorts of reasons. It's a nuisance, I know. I'm sure you'll be able to sort it out with the credit card company...'

Darren looks around him, sensing that the whole queue is now listening in on this, and then says: 'Look, it's my bloody card – give it here, now.'

Martin replies: 'Look, I'm really sorry, but I'm afraid I can't. I have to keep it; you see there's a procedure I have to follow.' Darren becomes very angry and clenches his fist saying: 'Don't give me that, you prat! Give me my bloody card or I'll come round there and get it myself.'

Martin says: 'I'm sorry, but this card could be stolen – I can't give it back to you and that's that!'

Enraged, Darren reaches over the counter and grabs Martin's shirt.

Darren bangs the counter and shouts: 'You will be sorry by the time I've finished with you …' He then reaches over the counter and grabs Martin by his shirt. As he does so, he sees that the security staff have been alerted and are running towards him, so he pushes Martin and runs for the exit.

The background to Martin's actions

Martin is 22 years old and has worked in retail for about three years. He doesn't particularly enjoy it, but it's a job and he can't think of much else he would like to do. Some days it can be interesting, but he finds the till work boring, and he just about manages to keep a friendly approach to the customers.

He saw this problem coming. He could see the customer was getting agitated about waiting, and he couldn't believe it when the card didn't work. He was also surprised that the customer got so angry so quickly – but there was no way he was giving the card back, not when the card company pays you £50 if you hold onto it.

The background to Darren's actions

Darren is 23 years old and considers himself to be pretty fit. Image is important to him and he likes to look good. The MP3 player was for his girlfriend's birthday, and he was about to meet her and take her out for a meal that evening.

They'd had a big row the night before about him going out with his mates, and he was now running late because he had stopped off for a pint on the way to meet her. He always seemed to end up in the wrong queue and was getting pretty wound up about being kept waiting.

He knew that he was well up to the limit on his card – well, probably over it – and they had warned him about it. The bloke at the counter couldn't be bothered, and when he wanted to keep the card as well – that made Darren flip.

Case study exercise:
The refused credit card

Look at the case study and list any triggers. Explain why they caused the situation to escalate.

De-escalating responses

Animals tend to respond automatically, fight or flight, when something happens. If you pull a dog's tail it is very likely that it will bite you. This is the dog's automatic reaction.

Humans are, however, different. People have a choice about how they respond to a threatening situation. At first the emotional side kicks in, with your body's fight or flight response. As the rational side catches up, you can then start to analyse the situation and respond more appropriately.

Right and wrong choices

Your choice is important because every choice has a consequence. Even when you have passed the 'fight or flight' stage you still have a choice between escalating or de-escalating the situation.

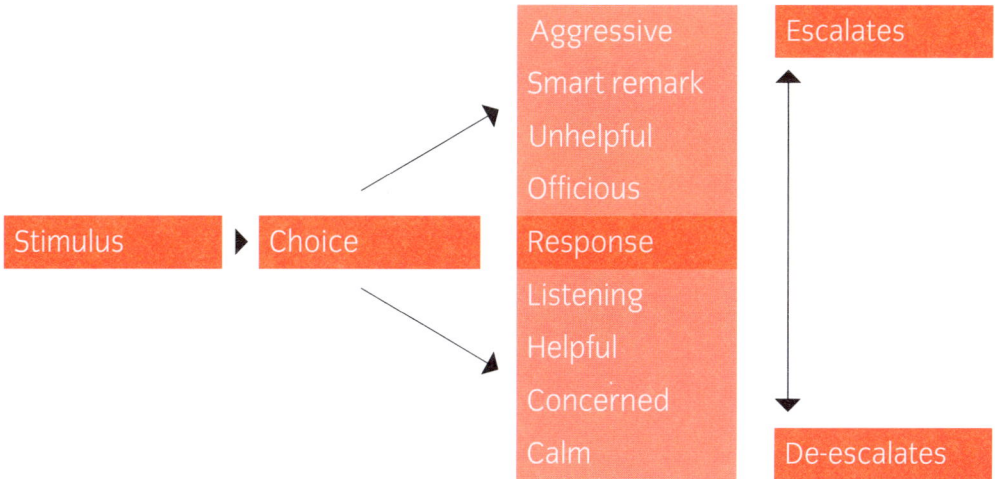

Every choice you make can escalate or de-escalate a given situation.

When you are feeling angry, emotional or tense, you might easily do something or say something that will make things worse. A smart comment or a pointing or poking finger could trigger an escalation. The wrong choice can escalate the problem.

You need to consciously choose to deal with the incident so that no one loses face or gets more wound up or frustrated.

Case study exercise:
The refused credit card

Look at the case study and think about how Martin dealt with Darren. What choices did he make about the way he decided to deal with him?

2 Avoiding and defusing conflict

Pro-active service delivery

Workplace conflict can occur for many different reasons. Some of the causes stem directly from the personal circumstances, control, health or wellbeing of the aggressor and are beyond the control of the organisation or staff who are confronting the individual concerned. Sometimes, however, organisations and staff can create or exacerbate the environment within which a conflict develops and increase the risk of violence by the way they deliver services or approach their work.

There is a build up to the majority of violent incidents, and often the most significant action that can be taken to reduce violence is to provide a high quality service. For example, customers, clients or patients can understandably become very frustrated over delays, cancellations or waiting times and usually it is the lack of information that fuels the frustration. When their frustration is not dealt with to that person's satisfaction, the situation can all too easily escalate. Providing timely information may be all that is needed to placate and calm agitated service users.

Making the right impression

Your first contact with your customers will create an impression. This impression begins with your appearance, facial expression and the way you are standing. In most cases your first contact with service users will be pleasant, welcoming, helpful and smiling. Your service users will then usually be equally pleasant. However, they may be frustrated, anxious, tired, excited, noisy, drunk or affected by drugs – whatever their condition, they are more likely to respond aggressively if you seem aggressive to them. Actively listening, which will be covered later, will help to develop positive communication with customers.

You can go a long way towards preventing many conflicts by:
- smiling and being pleasant and helpful
- looking and sounding professional
- acting consistently and fairly
- working effectively as a team.

If you behave professionally and are pleasant and helpful, you are less likely to become a target. Also you are more likely to get help from other service users if and when you need it. This is not a sign of weakness; it is a sign of confidence and strength.

Control your tone of voice

- speak clearly and in a controlled way. This will help people accept what you say
- do not raise your voice
- focus on facts rather than opinion
- avoid using critical or sneering tones in your voice
- never talk down to people.

Control your body language

Show you understand your service user's feelings by nodding and smiling. This also helps them to accept what you are saying or doing. If you slouch, fidget, avoid eye contact or appear distracted, people will think you are not comfortable talking to them. Make sure that your body language is saying 'I am in control of the situation and I am paying attention to you. You are important to me.' The following will help you do this:

- maintain natural eye contact: if you avoid looking people in the eye, you may appear nervous and not in control. Natural eye contact – but not staring – will help
- show attentiveness: engage with the other person and let them see you are ready to help
- look alert: concentrate on what is happening around you.

Case study: The missed train

Jenny Henderson is 53 years old, and married with four grown up children. She has 20 years of experience on the railways and works at Walford Station as one of the platform staff.

At 17:00 on Sunday 23 September, Jenny started her duties at Walford Station. There were other Platform Assistants working on other platforms. She'd had a very busy week and was looking forward to having two days off during the coming week.

At 22:55 Jenny had just despatched the last train out of Walford to Sandford and was preparing to finish her shift when she was approached by a member of the public, Sharon Moore, asking what time the next train to Sandford was due. Sharon is white, about 35 years of age, very thin build, and was wearing black trousers, blouse and a leather bomber-type jacket. She was out of breath, speaking very quickly and looked very agitated.

2 Avoiding and defusing conflict

Sharon grabbed Jenny's arm and twisted it.

Jenny said: 'I reckon you'll be walking love, your train left a couple of minutes ago. There aren't any more trains tonight.' Sharon became more agitated, insisting that there must be another train to get her home. She shouted: 'Listen, my kids are with a baby sitter, I've got to get back.' Jenny replied: 'Look, are you telling me I don't know my job? There aren't no trains, lady!'

There were only a couple of people in the area walking out of the station when Sharon grabbed Jenny's left arm and twisted her wrist, shouting: 'There's got to be a train, you silly cow.'

Jenny shouted: 'Get off me!' and managed to pull herself free. Sharon then stormed out of the station. A member of the security staff administered first aid to Jenny and treated her for a sprained and bruised wrist.

Jenny Henderson's view

I have been a Platform Assistant for about twenty years and have worked at Walford for the last five years. I suffer from a bad back, so some days I am really uncomfortable and I just want my shift to end. I've made a lot of friends and now the kids have grown up I like to get out of the house and see new people. The job's okay really, and most days I have a laugh. Some passengers think you can magic up a train or just hold it in the station until they are ready to catch it. It's never their fault, but half the time they've left it too late and then blame us!

I started my shift at 17:00 on Sunday 23 September. It started quite busy, but quietened down a bit later on in the evening. I was glad when the last train passed through and I could finish my shift. I was really tired and my back was playing me up.

Just as I was going to walk off the platform, this woman rushes up to me asking for the next train to Sandford. She must have seen it pull out of the station, and if she lived in Sandford she would have known when the last train left Walford.

If I'm honest, I don't like her type at all. It's obvious she was a tart and I can't stand people who just leave their kids with anybody so they can have a good time. No sense of responsibility – I worked hard and brought my four kids up, but I'd never have gone out and left them so late – they must be at school in the morning as well.

I might have been unhelpful by telling her she'd have to walk, but you know, what did she expect from me? It's not my fault if she's too busy doing other things to get to the station on time. She got really wound up and started shouting at me, insisting there must be a train. As if I'd not have told her if there had been one. I tell her there isn't one, and she grabs my arm and twists my wrist round, yelling at me like a mad woman. I shout for her to get off, and she storms out of the station.

The security guy had a look at my wrist and treated me for a bruised and sprained wrist. I just don't know why it happened. It all happened so fast.

Sharon Moore's view

I'd been to Walford to see my boyfriend. We haven't been getting on too well lately and needed to sort a few things out. We'd had a couple of bottles of wine and ended up having this massive row. I was really upset and didn't want to leave until we'd patched it up. I was a bit late calling the taxi and then it took longer than it should have. Anyway, the upshot was that I didn't get to the station until five to eleven. I was feeling really wound up by the time I got there.

I saw a train just pulling out; I didn't think it could have been mine as I thought I'd just made it. I had to get back before midnight because I had a young girl baby-sitting the kids and promised I'd be back. She's got school in the morning and so have my kids. I was really panicky; I kept trying to ring her, but the phone just kept ringing out. I didn't know whether she'd just left the kids and gone home or what. There was this woman in uniform walking off the platform, so I asked her when the next train was. She must have seen that I was out of breath because I'd run all the way from the taxi. She gives me this clever reply about me having to walk or something. Was she winding me up or what? I don't know what her problem was – I only asked about the next train!

I'm usually fairly calm, but she really wound me up, so I may have shouted at her. She put on this really snotty voice and put her hands on her hips. She looked at me like I was a piece of shit and just couldn't be bothered to help me. She just made me mad, so I grabbed her wrist and gave it a good twist. Well, she deserved it. I then went to find a taxi.

Case study exercise: The missed train

What sort of first impression did Jenny Henderson create?

Customer expectations and flashpoints

In any sector, there are always certain activities, incidents or times of day when frustration and anger are especially likely to occur. It is important to find out the main causes of frustration and flashpoints, and then with your management you can to take steps to reduce the risk of aggression.

It is also important to understand that your service user can have unrealistic expectations of the service you can provide. Queuing is a good example – most people expect to be dealt with quickly and professionally and therefore it creates frustration when they have to wait. You may not be able to change the situation but it is important to make contact quickly with each service user affected to explain what is happening and why – and how long they will be expected to wait. This will not resolve their problems but it helps to avoid the situation getting aggressive because the person's anger has slowly built up.

2 Avoiding and defusing conflict

Case study exercise: The missed train

In the case study, what are Sharon Moore's expectations (reasonable or otherwise)?

What are the realities of the situation?

What sort of things could Jenny Henderson have done to help to manage the gap between expectations and reality?

Behaviour breeds behaviour

It is extremely unlikely that you will have a positive attitude towards everyone you meet in the course of your work. If you are dealing with someone you feel negative towards, you are likely to show those negative feelings in the way that you behave towards the other person. This is shown in the Attitude and Behaviour Cycle.

The Attitude and Behaviour Cycle.

My attitude → Affects → My behaviour → Affects → Your attitude → Affects → Your behaviour → Affects → My attitude

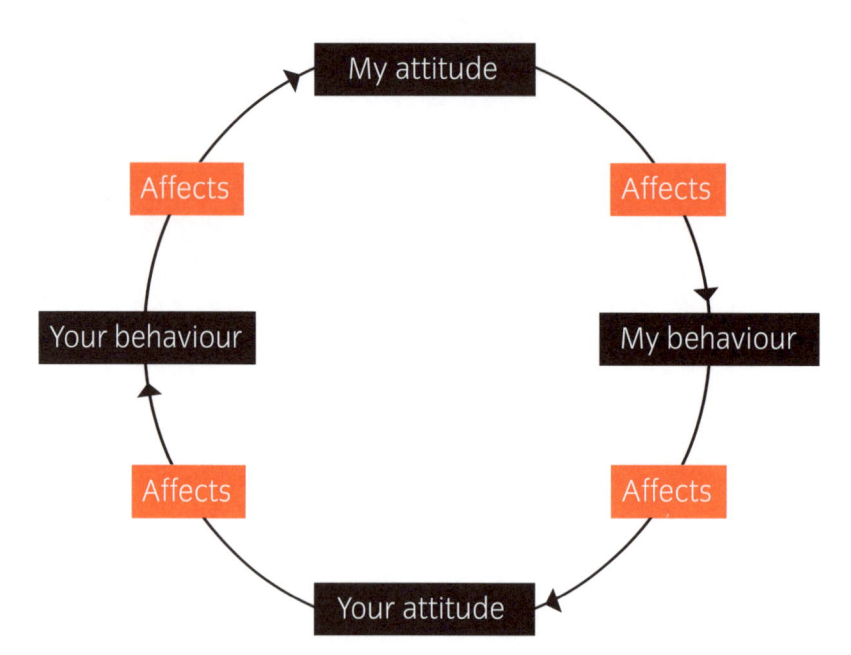

Your negative behaviour makes a situation worse

If you have a negative attitude towards someone, your unconscious behaviour will let that person know how you feel about him or her. When the other person recognises this negative behaviour from you, this will in turn affect their attitude towards you. A negative attitude will come out in their behaviour towards you. Their negative behaviour is then likely to make the negative feelings you had in the first place even more negative.

It is very difficult to change your attitude towards someone. It is, however, possible to change the way you behave towards them. You can learn to behave so that your negative feelings do not show, so that your behaviour doesn't reflect your negative feelings. This breaks the cycle and stops it getting worse. A positive attitude makes the cycle work the other way – producing positive behaviours, which in turn produce positive attitudes.

2 Avoiding and defusing conflict

Case study exercise: The missed train

Look at the case study. Write down the attitudes of Jenny Henderson, the Platform Assistant.

Write down the behaviours that Jenny is showing because of those attitudes.

Write down the attitudes of Sharon Moore that have developed because of this behaviour.

Write down the behaviour that Sharon shows because of it.

How could Jenny have prevented the situation from escalating?

Communication – and blocks to it

Communication is basically about getting an idea from your head into another person's head. This seems to be quite a simple process but it can be very difficult to convey the exact idea you want to get across to the other person.

Basics of communication

If telepathy were possible then there would be little problem – the whole idea in your mind would simply be transmitted across to the other person's mind – arriving in exactly the same state as it did when it left your mind.

The sender encodes and the receiver decodes.

Sender				Receiver
Encodes	▶	Message	▶	Decodes

In reality, it's not that simple. If you have an idea you have to find a way of getting it across to the other person. To do so, you have to break the idea down into something that you can 'send' and that the other person can 'receive'. You encode the idea – often into words but it may also be into a picture or some other representation – and send the 'message' to the other person. The other person receives the encoded message and then has to decode it and work out your original idea. This sounds straightforward, but it can be difficult and easily leads to misunderstanding.

These misunderstandings occur for many reasons – most of them are related to the fact that each of us sees our world in a very individual way. Our upbringing, values, experiences and culture mean that we are unique and can only see the world from our own point of view. Consequently, when you encode your message, you have to do it using your own assumptions and ways of seeing things. Similarly, when the receiver decodes it, he or she uses the same individual way of seeing the world to do so. Your worlds don't have to be too different for misunderstanding to occur.

2 Avoiding and defusing conflict

The misunderstood message.

"It's an animal. It's ginger coloured. It has black stripes, a long tail and pointed ears. It has whiskers and paws with..."

Of course, most communication is 'two-way' and usually, if you are not sure about the meaning of a message, you will 'check out' your understanding of what the intended message was. The 'sender – message – receiver' model has a second phase to it – 'feedback and check understanding'.

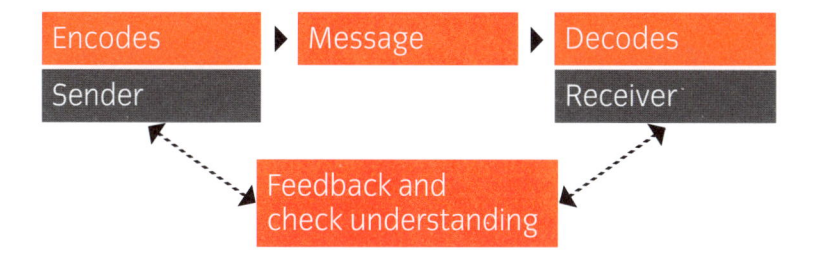

The sender and receiver offer feedback and check understanding.

The receiver has a responsibility to check out their understanding with the sender: 'Er... is this animal dangerous?' The sender also has a responsibility to ensure the message is being received: 'You look rather alarmed – do you not like tabby cats?'

Blocks to communication

A number of things can get in the way of good communication – these are termed 'blocks'. A block is anything that can cause the communication between two people to break down or become difficult.

The environment
The environment in which you are communicating can contain things that will have an effect upon the success of the communication. They are usually obvious – although you don't always recognise the effect they are having – and include:
- loud noise
- lots of people crowding together
- physical discomfort – feeling very hot or cold, being hungry or tired.

Emotion and feelings
When you are angry, frustrated or unhappy, the emotions generated will have a direct impact upon your ability to communicate successfully. You find it difficult to hear and correctly interpret words and tend to rely much more on the tone and body language to understand.

Alcohol and drugs
Alcohol has a depressant effect on the body, which results in slower reactions to normal stimulus. It tends to reduce people's inhibitions and can make them unreasonable and unpredictable.

When you are communicating with a person who is under the influence of alcohol:
- talk slowly and calmly
- adopt a non-aggressive stance
- maintain space between them and you.

There are many different drugs available and each can have a different effect on the person who has taken them. The effects can range from those similar to alcohol, to high stimulant effects and even hallucinations. The greatest communication difficulty is the unpredictability that can arise in people who have taken drugs and the fact that their world may be very distorted. The same points should be borne in mind as with alcohol but with greater emphasis on the need to demonstrate a non-aggressive stance and to maintain space between you and the other person. Remember, drugs and alcohol are often mixed and their effects can be difficult to predict.

Different cultures communicate differently

Different cultures hold different values and attitudes to define the way they live and interact with others. There are no 'rights' and 'wrongs' where culture is concerned – one culture isn't better than another – just different!

Some of this difference may be in things like body language; hand signs in one culture can mean something very different in another. The difference in space between people when communicating can vary from culture to culture. There are often differences in values, which are difficult to accept.

If you want to communicate well with someone who is clearly from a different cultural or ethnic background to yourself, then it is important to respect the values of that culture and try to communicate in a way that embraces those values as much as possible.

Mental health problems

Mental illness can take many forms and you will often have no idea that the person you are dealing with is suffering from a mental illness. A small percentage of people may have a more serious illness, which can cause them to be aggressive in some circumstances:
- fear and confusion (eg of noise or of people) leading to desperation and the feeling that 'the only way out is to fight'
- paranoia (feelings of being persecuted) may be directed towards certain groups in society, for example police or doctors, and could have been caused by bad experiences with them in the past
- anger at being provoked by other people.

When dealing with a person who has a mental illness:
- give him or her plenty of space
- talk clearly and calmly to ensure he or she understands you
- make sure he or she knows you mean no harm
- be reassuring. Tell him or her what you are doing and why
- keep your hands open and in view
- reduce distractions that will alarm or confuse
- if you are with a colleague, only one of you should talk to the person.

People with learning disabilities

People with learning disabilities experience the same emotions as other people and may become upset or angry when they are in an unfamiliar environment, especially when in pain or discomfort. They may also communicate in different ways, eg using symbols or pictures. Some have good expressive language but have great difficulty in understanding what is said to them, so it is very important not to assume they have understood.

Good things to remember:
- speak clearly and don't over-complicate language
- be sure to signal non-aggression
- one person should speak, in a calm way
- avoid having an audience or attracting a crowd as this may confuse or anger the person
- reassure the person that you are trying to help them – remember, to them you are a stranger. Empathise and be sensitive to their needs
- do not touch the person unless invited. For example, if someone is lost and scared they may want to hold your hand, while others may not welcome physical contact.

Some people with learning disabilities may behave in ways that are considered socially unusual, for example, rocking or biting their hand. This may be a coping strategy when stressed and should not be misinterpreted as a threat to you.

2 Avoiding and defusing conflict

Case study exercise:
The missed train

Write down all the blocks to communication you can identify in the case study.

Non-verbal communication

Channels of communication
In conversation the message is passed from one person to the other through three channels:
— words (the actual words spoken)
— tone (the way the words are spoken)
— non-verbal communication (signs such as stance, gestures and expressions).

Many studies have been done about communication, and it is generally accepted that in a face-to-face situation the receiver gains the meaning of a message mainly through non-verbal communication. Next in importance is tone. Last in importance is the words that are actually said. The relative importance of non-verbal communication, tone and words is shown in the diagram below.

Channels of communication.

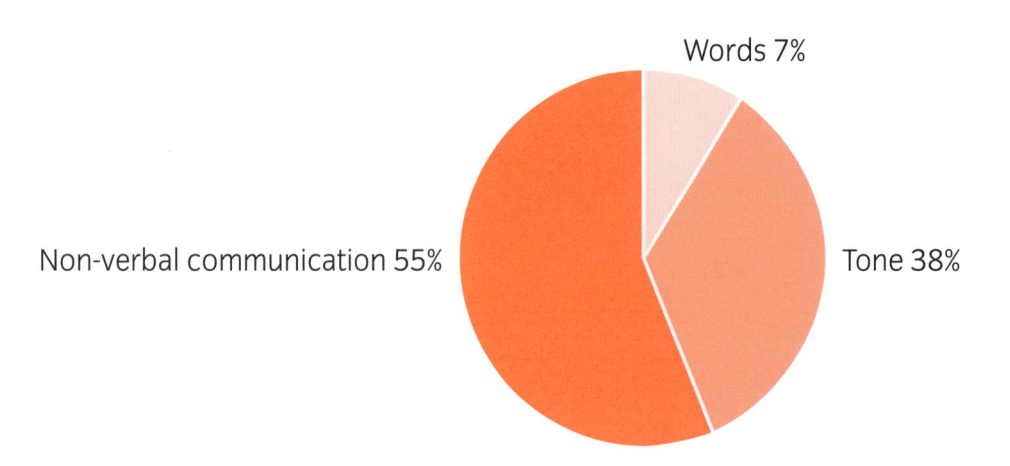

Words 7%
Tone 38%
Non-verbal communication 55%

We can easily use body language which signals anger, frustration or aggression without realising that we are doing it. It is important to be aware of our stance, posture, eye contact and gestures to avoid giving the wrong signals.

2 Avoiding and defusing conflict

Signalling non-aggression

Signalling aggression and non-aggression through body language.

This is one of the most important areas to understand when defusing a situation where people are becoming aggressive. The more emotional someone is becoming the less they can hear and rationalise what is being said to them. However, they will instinctively respond to body language and tone of voice.

Aggressive signals are easy to spot – as someone becomes angrier they tend to turn square on, stare fixedly and clench their fists. To signal that you are not aggressive you need to do the opposite. Turn slightly to the side, one shoulder turned away, open palms and normal eye contact.

Open palms

An open-handed gesture is a very powerful signal that you don't want to fight. It is connected with the reason why we shake hands in greeting. (This originated in the times when people always carried weapons. When approaching someone they used to show an extended open right palm to prove they were not threatening the other person with a weapon. This slowly changed into a handshake.)

Eye contact and active listening

Eye contact is a vital element in signalling non-aggression. In a normal conversation, the listener will maintain eye contact with the speaker. The speaker will drop eye contact from time to time. In aggressive situations it is important to try to achieve as near normal eye contact as possible. Never stare fixedly at the other person, as this can feel very aggressive. It is also important to recognise that 'normal' eye contact may differ across cultures. For example, in some cultures it is a sign of disrespect to look directly into the eyes of someone in authority. In another culture, that same lack of eye contact may be seen as looking guilty, 'shifty' or nor telling the truth. It's not hard to imagine the resulting misunderstanding in an interaction between two people from these different cultures – one person is trying to say 'I'm showing respect' and the other is interpreting it as 'you look shifty to me'.

In 'active listening' we demonstrate with head nodding, gestures and repeating back phrases that we are hearing and understanding what the other person is saying.

Space

We have three basic 'zones' of space. The distances shown for these zones are averages and can vary quite a lot from person to person. Distances also vary between cultures. Most of us are only comfortable with close family or partners in our intimate zone. If someone is trying to intimidate or threaten you, he or she will attempt to move into your intimate space.

Zones of space around a person.

Stranger space
1.2–3 metres

Normal space
0.5–1.2 metres

Intimate space
0–0.5 metres

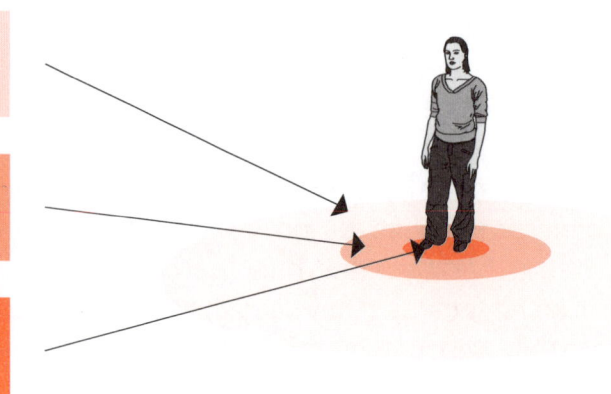

2 Avoiding and defusing conflict

There are various ways to create and measure personal space:
- Can you see the other person's feet, at least in your peripheral vision?
- Would they have to take a step forward in order to touch (hit) you?
- If someone is in your intimate space it is very noticeable – you may feel physically uncomfortable, trapped, unsafe or threatened.

Stance

In normal circumstances we rarely stand 'square on' to someone when we speak to them. We tend to stand slightly to one side. When we become aggressive we tend to stand fairly close up and 'square on' to the other person. In a situation where you recognise that the aggression is increasing, ensure that you are not standing 'square on' by dropping one foot backwards, allowing your shoulder to 'drop away'. This also opens up visual 'exit routes' for both you and the other person.

Signal non-aggression and open up exit routes.

Dealing with high-risk conflict

Sometimes, despite your best efforts at defusing the situation, it will be clear that the incident is escalating to a point where you are in danger of being physically assaulted. This is a 'high-risk conflict'. If you find yourself in a high-risk conflict then you should remove yourself from that situation as soon as you can safely do so.

There are also occasions where you have 'bitten': the situation has become personal and you are being sucked into the escalation. Again, you should seek to leave the situation as soon as you can or hand over to a colleague.

Levels of escalation

Anger has a similar effect on people as fear. The body is 'geared up' for action. This is why people who are angry can become violent so quickly. It is important to understand how frustration can lead to violence. The path of escalation can be traced through four levels:

Level 4 Violence	The highest level of arousal occurs when the aggression spills over into violence and the other party is physically assaulted by the aggressor.
Level 3 Aggression	At the next level, the anger is turned towards the other party. The aggression will be evident through voice level, tone, verbal and non-verbal behaviour.
Level 2 Anger	Anger is a deeper level of emotion and will be fairly obvious to an observer. If controlled, it will not be directed specifically at the other party but the individual will be less rational.
Level 1 Frustration	Most conflict involves a degree of frustration and this forms the lowest level of arousal. It may not be evident or obvious, and the individual can keep it very much under control.

Most aggressors will stay in the same level unless something happens that triggers the person into the next level of escalation. To avoid escalation, we need to try to keep the person at the same level and preferably to take them down to a lower level of arousal. This means, first of all, avoiding any comments or behaviour that are likely to trigger the person into the next level – and secondly to employ the calming techniques covered later in this book.

When dealing with someone in a conflict situation, we can't be sure what level of arousal he or she is in. He or she may be having a bad day, or may be worried or frustrated about something that has nothing to do with you. By the time the person meets you, he or she may already be in Level 2 and, if triggered, will escalate to the aggression of Level 3 and turn it towards you.

Signs of escalation

You need to recognise when a situation is escalating and respond appropriately. Signs to watch out for include:
- angry non-verbal signals (face reddening, intense eye contact, angry facial features)
- abuse which is focused on you personally
- increasingly vulgar, abusive or threatening language
- your personal space is being invaded
- square on posture, head and chin thrust forward
- fist clenching
- finger pointing, leading to physical contact.

John Parker tumbles to the ground.

Case study: The parking incident

John Parker is a successful businessman living in Surrey. He has a very important business meeting at 10.00 am at a hotel in Leicester. He decides to drive there. He intends to leave at 6.00 am and arrive about 8.30 am – in good time to have a light breakfast and read his notes before the meeting.

He wakes suddenly and sees that it is 6.00 am – he has set the alarm incorrectly. He jumps out of bed and dashes quickly into the shower, dresses and jumps into his car. It's raining heavily and he drives as quickly as he dares but gets stuck in a set of road works. He arrives in Leicester at 9.00 am. He only has time for a coffee and finds a car parking space with a 30-minute stay. He decides this is enough time and sets off to find a café. This proves more difficult than he expects, and he eventually joins a queue in a coffee shop, gets served and sits down to his coffee and meeting notes at 9.20 am. He gulps down his coffee and leaves the shop at 9.30 am. He walks very quickly, but is confident that it's unlikely a parking attendant will have spotted his car. He turns into the street at 9.45 am and sees a parking attendant standing by his car writing in what appears to be a notebook. John is sweating and breathing so hard that he can barely speak.

Gilbert Roberts is the parking attendant. He hates the early shift, but he believes in being professional and has never been late for work. He sees John Parker running towards him and has a bet with himself that this is his car. Fifteen minutes over time and he deserves a ticket is Gilbert's view.

John manages to blurt out: 'You haven't written the ticket yet, have you?'

Roberts: 'No, sir, but it won't take me a minute.'

Parker: 'Come on, mate, give us a break. Surely you can let me off. I've had a really crap morning and I've got an important meeting in a few minutes.'

Roberts: 'Listen, I'm not your "mate", and I'm afraid I can't do anything about it. A couple of minutes, maybe – but fifteen minutes is well over.'

Parker: 'You don't have to write it – I've been this much over before and your mates have let me off. It's only my bad luck that you're snooping round here just as my time runs out.'

Roberts: 'I think I know my job, sir. I won't be more than a couple of minutes if you'll just keep quiet and let me write this out.'

Parker moves closer to Roberts and bangs his fist down on the roof of his car – pointing his finger at Roberts. He shouts: 'Listen you – don't be such a smart arse. You're a waste of space. A bit of power and you think you can treat people like shit!'

Roberts: 'Okay, sir, I've had enough of this. I'm afraid your behaviour is unacceptable – I'm going to call for some assistance.'

Parker lunges forward and grabs hold of Roberts by his shirt, shouting: 'It's an ambulance you'll be needing before I've finished with you.' Roberts struggles with Parker for a second and then gives him a hard push. Parker releases his grip on Roberts' shirt and tumbles backwards against the car, falling heavily to the ground.

Case study exercise: The parking incident

In the case study, what level of escalation was Parker in as he arrived back at his car?

At what points did he move into the next levels and what were the triggers?

What were the signs that the incident was escalating?

Strategies for defusing aggressive behaviour

The best course of action when confronted with aggressive behaviour is to withdraw from the situation. However, there are many occasions when this is not possible. For example, you may have other vulnerable service users around who may be in danger or it may not be possible to exit safely from the incident. If this is the case, then it is important to be able to defuse the situation and calm the aggressor. There are strategies that you can employ to defuse the situation. These are essential tools in high-risk situations.

Maintain self-control

It is vitally important to maintain your self-control and not to 'bite', that is, not to be pulled into a conflict. An angry customer may try to 'pull you in' and may well use personal abuse, personal attack, vulgar or unpleasant language and very threatening gestures.

Try to retain your 'state of independence' and not be drawn in. It may help if you think of it this way – if you become angry, lose it or bite – who has won? Clearly the customer has. This is probably what the angry customer has been trying to do, and if you get angry, then the customer has achieved what he or she set out to do.

Signal non-aggression

It is important to catch the person's attention and give signals which will calm and de-escalate the situation. The most important thing to signal here is non-aggression.

Match energy levels

It is important to match the energy level of the other person. If you are slow to respond, or respond too calmly, it can give the impression that you don't care or aren't really interested in the other person's problem or issue. Matching energy does not mean that you should be 'aggressive' back to the other person – it means that you should quickly engage with him or her and demonstrate with your body language and tone that you are concerned and interested.

Show empathy and listen actively

You need to be an active listener. Don't assume you already know what people are going to say. The customer will respond to signs that you are listening and understanding his or her problem. This isn't the same as agreeing with his or her point of view. Use phrases like:

'I can understand why this has made you angry' or 'I can see why this is frustrating for you'.

In order to reassure a customer that you are really listening to what they are saying, it is important to:
- focus your attention on them
- use non-verbal cues (eg nodding the head)
- show that you have understood. Say things like: 'Okay, let me see if I've understood you correctly' and then paraphrase what they have said
- maintain appropriate eye contact. This reinforces the non-verbal message that you are paying attention to what is being said
- let them finish speaking before you act. Try not to interrupt or cut across a person's speech.

When someone is in a high state of emotion and anger, there is little point in trying to appeal to their rational side. Saying things like 'Let me explain…' or 'The reason why we have this rule is …' will probably only make things worse and increase their anger.

Appeal to the rational side later. When you have re-established the balance and the customer is less emotional, you can begin to work on their rational side and start to resolve the problem.

Win his or her trust

Winning trust is getting the person to the point where he or she is calm enough to be able to deal with the situation in a rational manner. He or she has to have confidence that you are 'on their side', want to resolve the problem and have some power to be able to resolve the situation. If you have successfully negotiated the first three steps, then you will have reached this point.

Recognise the other person's point of view

It is important to try to remove the cause of the problem that has led to the conflict. This can only be achieved when the 'heat' is out of the situation and everyone is thinking rationally. Remember that the customer will have a different point of view to you – otherwise the conflict would not have started in the first place.

It can be quite difficult to recognise the other points of view in a particular situation. This may be because you have a different set of values to the other person, or because you have different goals or interests in the outcome. You will think that you are right in your view – but you have to remember that the other person will believe they are right. If this wasn't the case then you wouldn't have any conflict!

This can be understood by looking at the following shapes:

They are all exactly the same thing. How can this be?

People may have different points of view.

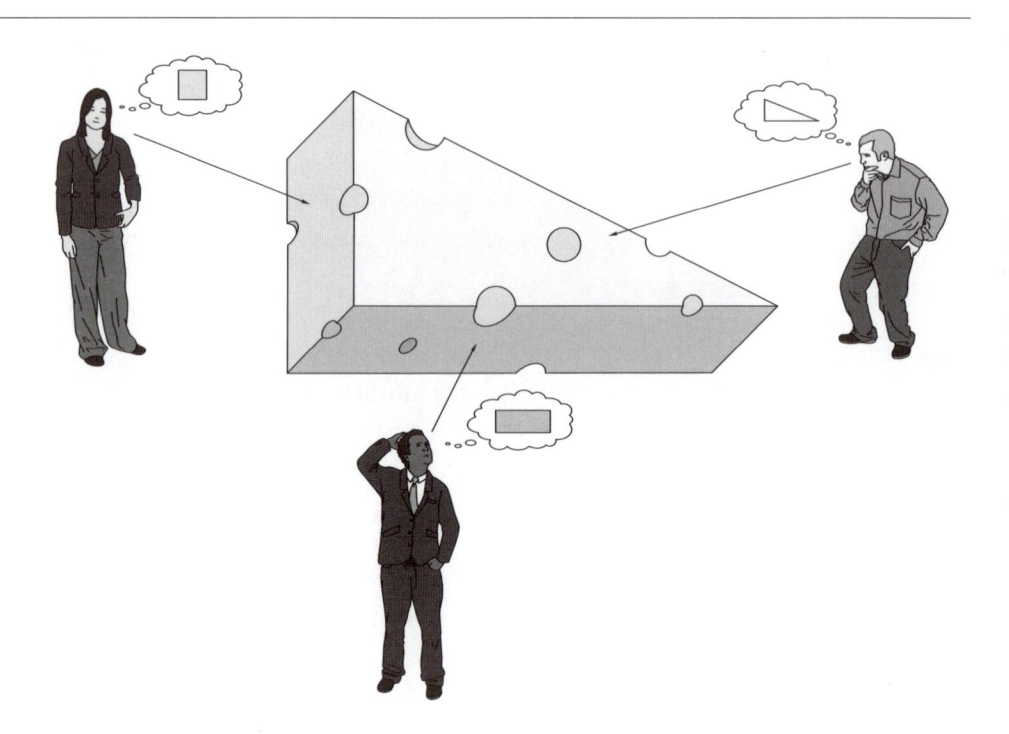

They are different views of a piece of cheese! It is important to able to see another person's point of view – even if you don't agree with it. Person A sees a square, Person B sees a triangle, Person C sees a rectangle, all very different shapes but actually views of the same thing – a wedge of cheese.

If you look at the wedge of cheese as the 'problem' it becomes clear that people can have quite different beliefs about the same problem – depending upon their point of view. Each belief is correct to the individual – just a different point of view. The critical element is to understand that all involved believe that they are right. The more passionate people are about the issue, the more emotional they can become and the more entrenched they are in their view. The key to unlocking this problem is for one person to seek to listen and understand the other's point of view. Listening and positively seeking to understand provides the following benefits:
- as you are not resisting or arguing, the conflict can diminish
- listening to the other person shows that you are interested and care
- you can scan and assess your options while they are talking
- you may discover that the facts, or perceived facts, are different to your initial thoughts.

Seek a win–win outcome

To successfully resolve a situation we need to think 'win–win'. A 'win–win' situation is where both sides of a confrontation come out of the situation feeling satisfied with the outcome. To achieve it you need to:
- avoid criticism. Accept that the conflict is behind you and that you don't want to get back into it
- deal with the problem. Break down the issue into small parts and show that you can reach agreement.

Look for a 'win–win' solution – it is not always possible to meet everyone's ideal result, but if partly reached, people are more likely to be satisfied with their treatment. A simple explanation may be enough.

Case study exercise: The parking incident

Looking at the case study, write down the way that it might have gone if Roberts had recognised the situation and employed strategies for defusing aggressive behaviour.

Confronting unacceptable behaviour

It is very likely that at some time you will have to deal with someone whose behaviour is 'unacceptable'. They may be shouting and swearing, making it very difficult for you to do your job and upsetting other customers. Even in these difficult circumstances, you have options that you need to weigh up.

You have a choice about whether to confront

Remember that you always have a choice about whether or not to confront their behaviour. Confronting can easily lead to the escalation of an already difficult and risky situation. The last thing you want to do is make it worse. It is usually down to a personal choice and some abuse – particularly if it is very personal – can be difficult to let pass.

You can confront a problem when everyone is calmer

A problem doesn't have to be tackled when the other person is still angry or aggressive. When things have calmed down, you may want to confront the individual about their unacceptable behaviour. Indeed, the person will often recognise that he or she has been way out of line and will apologise for his or her behaviour before being confronted about it.

If you have to confront, do it assertively – not aggressively

If, for whatever reason, you decide to confront, then it is important to approach it in a way that will minimise the possible escalation. Many people make the mistake of thinking assertive behaviour is similar to aggressive behaviour. Acting angrily or aggressively will inevitably make things worse, and you need to ensure you confront the person about their behaviour in an assertive way. This gives them alternatives and lets them know you want to resolve the situation.

An example of a good assertive statement is: 'I appreciate you are angry, but if you continue to shout and swear, you leave me no option but to ask you to leave – which I don't want to have to do.'

Assertiveness is aimed at a person's behaviour rather than the person – as personal criticism can increase the likelihood of violence or aggression.

It shows empathy with the individual, respects the other person's position but clearly states what is unacceptable and what will happen if the unacceptable behaviour doesn't stop.

It is important to make sure your body language gives a similar message – you can make a good assertive statement but make it aggressive by squaring on or pointing. Remember to signal non-aggression.

Exit strategies

When you are in a situation that you recognise as high risk, it may be necessary for you to exit from the situation. This is to take yourself out of immediate danger and to allow you to think rationally about how to deal with the incident. People often find it difficult to get out of such situations without 'losing face' and therefore stay longer than it is safe to do so. An 'exit strategy' is a pre-prepared way of getting yourself away from a difficult situation.

Have a ready-made reason to exit
An 'exit strategy' is quite simply a sensible reason for leaving the situation you are in. You need to have a reason ready so that it comes to mind quickly. It needs to be something that will not make the situation worse.

It will be something like: 'I'm afraid I can't make that decision – I'll have to go and speak with the manager about it.'

Case study exercise: The parking incident

How could Roberts have improved the way he confronted the unacceptable behaviour from Parker?

The law relating to self-defence

The law relating to self-defence is reasonably clear and unambiguous.

The Common Law states that:

Any person may use such force as is reasonable in the circumstances in defence of themselves or others and, in certain circumstances, in defence of property.

The force used must be reasonable and no more than is necessary to repel the attack.

We must be able to show an honestly held belief that immediate unlawful personal violence was occurring or about to occur and our actions were necessary to prevent such conduct.

While the law is clear, society has a curious attitude towards 'defending oneself and one's property', which probably has its origins in the playground – 'If I hit you, you can hit me back'. This is reinforced by some parents who, when their son arrives home with a black eye, send him off to find the culprit and do the same to him.

As a consequence, confusion develops about the legitimacy of retaliation as opposed to self-defence. This has been highlighted recently by the case of the Norfolk farmer who shot a young man dead while he was climbing out of the window of his house, and other similar cases. It is important to realise that, whatever your personal feelings are about such incidents, they do not constitute 'lawful self-defence'. The law does not allow us to retaliate – only to defend ourselves from attack.

This confusion extends to the workplace, where employees who are faced with angry and violent customers take retaliatory action – rather than action that can be regarded as self-defence. Many people would say: 'If someone spits at me, I couldn't help but punch him back!' Although spitting is a disgusting act, it would be very difficult to justify a resulting punch in terms of self-defence.

Case study exercise: The parking incident

Was Roberts' final response a lawful use of force? Explain your reasoning.

3 Post-incident support and learning

Support for the victims **Case study: The nightclub incident**	69
Reporting an incident and accounting for your actions	74
Learning from what happened	76
Personal action plan	78
Helpful websites	79

Conflict Management in the Workplace

Outcome 3

Outcome 3 of the City & Guilds Level 2 Certificate in Conflict Management is set out below. It spells out what you need to do and what you need to know to successfully complete the part of the qualification.

Outcome 3
Identify post-incident support and report the circumstances to provide information for personal and organisation learning

What you need to do

- Report and record an incident of workplace violence to provide information to increase the prevention and reduction of risk across the organisation
- Review the incident, including the sequence of events leading up to it, to provide personal learning and the sharing of good practice with work colleagues
- Develop a personal action plan to ensure that he/she will deal more effectively with a similar incident

What you need to know

- Describe the reactions which may be experienced by a victim of workplace violence and the support mechanisms available for that person

3 Post-incident support and learning

Support for the victims

You may already have had experience of workplace violence, or your friends or colleagues may have been confronted by such aggression. Once the incident itself is over, the person who has experienced workplace violence needs support. Knowing about victim support could help you, and enable you to help others.

Case study: The nightclub incident

The woman head-butted Stephen full in the face.

Stephen Berrisford is a paramedic in the ambulance service with 15 years' service. He is 39 years old, 6'3" (190 cm) and married with four children. Amra Akrabati is an ambulance technician. He is 25 years old, 5'11" (180 cm) and single.

On Friday 23 August Stephen and Amra were working together on a 19:00 to 07:00 shift. They were having a very busy shift, which made the time go fast, but they had only managed to take a 15-minute break all night.

At 01:00 they were directed to Jolly's Night Club, where control reported there had been a large fight with the police in attendance. One person was reported to have head injuries. Stephen and Amra both hate attending this sort of incident as they usually receive grief from everyone around.

Amra, who was driving, pulled up as close to the nightclub as possible. They locked the ambulance and walked to the front of the club. There were four or five door staff milling around preventing anyone from entering or leaving the club. There was a lot of shouting going on. Two females were in handcuffs and being restrained by police officers. There was a man on the floor with obvious head injuries and blood over his face, clothes and the pavement. There were about 10 to 15 other people around pushing and shouting and generally trying to wind up the remaining police officers. Due to the continuing fracas it was impossible for Amra or Stephen to get to the man.

One of the females in handcuffs was kicking out at another police officer, who was restraining a second female in handcuffs. The officer asked Stephen to hold onto the female, while she went to assist her colleague. The handcuffed female that Stephen was asked to hold on to was about 19 years old, well built and about 5'10" (177 cm) tall.

Stephen was standing behind the female and was holding onto her left arm with his right hand. She said, 'Get your bloody hands off me, you're not a copper – mind your own business and piss off.' She tried to pull away, but Stephen was bigger and stronger than her and could easily hold her. Amra was standing to the right of Stephen and was keeping an eye on all the other action taking place.

The female Stephen was holding continued to be abusive, struggling to get free from Stephen's hold. He had a good grip and was confident she couldn't get away. All of a sudden the female threw her head back, head-butting Stephen full in the face, splitting his nose and causing it to bleed profusely. Stephen grabbed his face and Amra immediately took hold of the female, who was laughing and saying 'Serves you right – wanker'. Amra shouted to a nearby police officer to come and help.

Amra helped Stephen back to the ambulance, where he administered first aid. He then contacted control, requesting another ambulance to deal with the injured man.

3 Post-incident support and learning

Case study exercise: The nightclub incident

Write down the reactions that Stephen may be feeling immediately after the incident.

What reactions might he have on the day following the incident?

The affects of workplace violence

Perhaps the most important thing to recognise is that everyone has a different way of responding to and dealing with the aftermath of a violent or aggressive incident. There is no 'right' or 'wrong' way to react and people must be allowed to deal with it in their own way. Having said that, it is possible to categorise a range of typical reactions that may follow when someone has become the victim of an incident. They fall into three time periods; understanding these different reactions is helpful when supporting someone through the different stages of recovering from the incident.

The stages of recovery from a violent incident.

Short term	Medium term	Long term
24 hours	1 – 3 days	Weeks, months – possibly years

The time periods are very general and will vary according to the severity of the incident, the personal resilience of the people involved and the quality of the support they receive.

Short-term reactions
In the first few hours following the incident, the victim will have some initial reactions to the aggression and violence experienced. These reactions are predominantly emotional and are a direct response to the incident. Many factors will influence the severity of the reaction, not least of which is the individual's level of resilience towards traumatic situations.

The level of aggression, suddenness of the confrontation and physical injury sustained are also some of the factors that will influence how the victim will react. The following are the most likely:
– shock, confusion, disbelief, fear, helplessness
– anger, embarrassment, feeling of violation.

Many initial reactions will lessen as the victim moves into the next phase.

Medium-term reactions
The short-term reactions are characterised by their 'emotional' nature, formed before the victim has had time to think about, and begin to rationalise, what has happened. The medium-term reactions begin to appear when the victim has had a chance to consider the incident, to work through what happened and to think about the consequences, near misses and alternatives. This will be around 24 hours after the incident.

Reactions can include:
- feelings of loss, guilt, shame, embarrassment, humiliation
- exhaustion and tiredness
- denial of effects, ready to get back to work
- anger, frustration and resentment
- lack of confidence, anxiety about similar situations or meeting the aggressor.

Moving successfully through this medium-term phase is often the key to recovery. Once the victim has acknowledged what has happened and come to terms with it, he or she can then move back towards a normal life. Line managers can provide vital support in this phase and are pivotal in the successful recovery of most victims.

Long-term reactions
Generally, reactions that persist beyond a couple of weeks after the incident are indicative that the victim is finding difficulty in coming to terms with the incident and that he or she probably needs professional specialist help. Examples include:
- persistent tiredness, exhaustion, depression, bouts of anxiety
- excessive drinking and smoking, antisocial behaviour, irritable and aggressive behaviour
- nightmares, flashbacks, headaches, nausea, difficulty in eating and sleeping.

A victim who displays these long-term reactions clearly needs specialised help, and the employer should have mechanisms in place to detect this need and to provide access to appropriate help such as counselling, psychiatric or psychological services.

Employers should provide access to specialist help if required. This should include a counselling service and access to specialist psychological and psychiatric services in the rare event that they may be necessary. Larger employers are likely to have a formal employee assistance programme.

Colleagues can help by 'looking out' for someone who has been subjected to an assault. It is important to watch for changes in behaviour from what you would expect for this person. Remember, however, that everyone has a different way of responding to and dealing with the aftermath of a violent or aggressive incident. There is no right or wrong way to react and people must be allowed to deal with it in their own way.

Reporting an incident and accounting for your actions

Central to the risk assessment process is the incident reporting system. An important aspect of learning from what happened is to be able to accurately record the events. This means you will be able to reflect upon the incident and think about what you did well and how you might be able to improve things next time. It also means that you can account for the actions that you took. Finally, it means you can share good practice and help the organisation to learn from the incident.

As a professional you will be asked to account for your actions, or inaction, by your manager, and you could be called before a civil or criminal court months after the event. It is therefore very important to write a clear, detailed incident report immediately after an incident.

When writing your report, remember the ordinary person who was not present at the time of the incident, but who may be sitting on a jury in court. Ensure you provide enough detail for a third party to conclude that your actions were reasonable in the circumstances.

Help others to see the incident as it was and to understand how it felt being there. Give a true, accurate and full picture of what happened that would help others understand why you took the action that you did. This may sound like 'more paperwork', but it is for your benefit – one day you might be very glad that you took the time.

When completing your incident report remember to include:
- facts about yourself and the other party
- background information
- description of behaviour
- level of any force used, for example, in self-defence.

Simply stating that a person became 'abusive' or 'violent' is not satisfactory – state exactly what the person said, and what they did.

Reporting all incidents is essential in order to protect staff against risk. The organisation relies upon quality information to establish effective strategies and training. Reporting incidents of workplace violence is a duty under Health and Safety legislation.

Remember the definition of work-related violence: Any incident in which a person is abused, threatened or assaulted in circumstances relating to their work.

Given how broad this definition is, many people say that they would be putting a report in every few minutes if they were to report every incidence of verbal abuse they receive. Our personal levels of tolerance and our own definitions of 'threat' and 'abuse' make it difficult to set hard and fast rules – one person may feel threatened or abused in one incident where another wouldn't see the problem. Reporting should be encouraged and a report should be made of any incident which gives an individual, or his or her colleagues, cause for concern.

The Reporting of Injuries, Diseases and Dangerous Occurrences Regulations 1995 (RIDDOR)

Under these regulations employers must notify their enforcing authority in the event of an accident at work to any employee resulting in death, major injury or incapacity for normal work for three or more days. This includes any act of non-consensual physical violence done to a person at work.

Learning from what happened

As a professional, you should continuously be recognising the things that you do well in situations of conflict and looking for things that you might be able to do better in a similar incident. You should review how you approached the incident using this simple process:
- What happened?
- Why did it happen and go the way that it did?
- How can I improve things if this happens again?

There is no excuse for abusive or aggressive behaviour by a service user and it is important to avoid placing any blame on a victim in any incident of work-related violence. However, going through this process of reflection will help to ensure that you can stay as safe as possible if a similar incident should happen in the future.

3 Post-incident support and learning

Case study exercise: The night club incident

Look at the case study and write down things that Stephen might learn from the incident that will help him in a similar situation.

What things might Amra learn from it?

Write down the things that the ambulance service should learn from the incident.

Sharing good practice

You should make sure that you share your learning with your colleagues. Find out what they would have done in the same situation.

Feed information to your managers and try to look for long-term solutions to things. In particular, try to identify the problems that seem to re-occur. It could mean that a procedure, policy or rule is not reasonable or effective.

You might have information about a particular individual or group of people who have been identified as particularly difficult or threatening. You could also include effective ways that you have found for solving particular problems.

Personal action plan

Now that you have studied the issues of managing conflict, you will be more aware of the ways in which conflict develops and the strategies, skills and attitudes that will be effective in dealing with it. It is important to take some time to reflect upon what you have learned and to consider how you will use this learning to improve the way you manage the conflict that you meet.

What do you consider to be your main strength(s) in the way you handle conflict?

_____

_____

_____

What do you consider to be your main weakness(es) in the way you handle conflict?

_____

_____

_____

What have you learned from this programme that you feel will help you to deal with conflict more effectively?

_____

_____

_____

How will you put this into practice the next time you deal with a difficult person?

_____

_____

_____

3 Post-incident support and learning

Helpful websites

This workbook has provided you with a general view of the issues and problems around conflict management and work-related violence. The following websites will provide you with more detailed information about some of the topics you have looked at and about the specific issues of particular sectors.

City & Guilds www.cityandguilds.com
The City & Guilds website can give you more information on Conflict Management and related qualifications, including how it can provide partial exemption within the Level 2 Certificate for Security Guards and the Level 2 National Certificate for Door Supervisors. In addition, City & Guilds offers a range of different professional and vocational qualifications to help you to further your personal or career development.

British Crime Survey www.homeoffice.gov.uk/rds/bcs1.html
The most informative source of statistical information is the British Crime Survey, which conducts a yearly survey into a broad range of crime-related topics, including workplace violence.

Department of Health www.doh.gov.uk
The Department of Health website hosts the National Task Force on Violence against Health Care Staff.

Health and Safety Executive www.hse.gov.uk
The HSE website is very comprehensive and contains lots of informative data and links to more specialised help and advice about issues of policy, risk assessment and reduction. The HSE also provides a range of sector-specific publications, which deal with the specific issues of workplace violence in particular organisations.

Institute of Conflict Management www.conflictmanagement.org/icmn
The ICM mission statement is: 'To develop, monitor and promote professional standards for the effective prevention and management of aggression and conflict at work and to achieve pre-eminence as the national lead body for the setting of standards and accreditation of conflict management training and related services in all sectors.' Their website is useful for up-to-date information about standards across the sectors and issues relating to conflict management, conferences, reports, media items and research.

Maybo Ltd www.maybo.com
Maybo is a leading UK specialist in the management of conflict and violence in the workplace. Their pioneering work is helping hundreds of organisations to manage these issues effectively. The company specialises in working with organisations to tailor a complete solution to cater for their specific needs across the whole area of managing work-related violence.

National Health Service www.nhs.uk www.cfsms.nhs.uk
The NHS has been at the forefront of many initiatives relating to workplace violence. Perhaps the most widely publicised was the 'Zero Tolerance' campaign, which forms the basis of the Security Management Service. The NHS website is a mine of useful information about the practical ways that security issues can be approached across the sector. Much of the information, advice and guidance is transferable across to other sectors.

Suzy Lamplugh Trust www.suzylamplugh.org
The Suzy Lamplugh Trust, a registered charity, is a leading authority and campaigner on personal safety issues. The organisation provides a wealth of information, advice and guidance about all aspects of work-related violence, together with training aids, books, booklets, videos, packs, programmes and personal safety attack alarms.

Trades Union Congress www.tuc.org.uk
TUC Online has a searchable database of press releases, documents, fact sheets and conference and congress reports, which will provide up-to-date information about the issues. The site also provides links to the sector-specific unions who provide advice, guidance and help about the issues of work-related violence in specific roles.

UK Online www.ukonline.gov.uk
This website is a general gateway into any information, statistics, research, reports or press releases concerning national and local government.

Victim Support www.victimsupport.com
Victim Support is the independent charity that helps people cope with the effects of crime. It provides free and confidential support and information to help people deal with their experience. It is a very comprehensive 'one stop shop' for information, advice and guidance for the support of victims and witnesses who have been involved in crime.